DEMYSTIFYING AFFILIATE MARKETING

Unveiling the Path to Profitable Partnerships

JACK STEWART

Disclaimer:

The information provided in this book is for educational and informational purposes only. The author and publisher of this book are not engaged in rendering legal, financial, or professional advice. While every effort has been made to ensure the accuracy, completeness, and currency of the information presented, neither the author nor the publisher assumes any responsibility for errors or omissions, or for any outcomes resulting from the use of the information provided in this book.

The strategies, techniques, and recommendations discussed in this book are not guaranteed to generate specific results. Every individual's success in affiliate marketing depends on their own skills, efforts, and circumstances. It is recommended that readers consult with professionals, such as legal or

Table of content

Introduction to Affiliate Marketing

Welcome to the realm of boundless opportunity – the universe of Affiliate Marketing. Imagine a world where collaboration fuels prosperity, where businesses and individuals join forces not out of obligation, but out of shared ambition. This is the essence of Affiliate Marketing – a dynamic landscape where innovation, strategy, and determination converge to unlock unparalleled success.

In this journey of discovery, we will unveil the intricate tapestry of Affiliate Marketing, unraveling its threads to reveal how it has transformed from a mere concept to a thriving ecosystem that powers businesses and empowers individuals. As we embark on this odyssey, prepare to be immersed in the fundamentals, history, and undeniable relevance of Affiliate Marketing in today's digital age.

Hold onto the reins of your curiosity as we traverse through the corridors of this guide, shedding light on the very essence of Affiliate Marketing. Brace yourself for insights that transcend the ordinary, strategies that redefine the possible, and stories that bear testament to the extraordinary power of collaboration. Whether you're a seasoned entrepreneur seeking new avenues or an aspiring affiliate navigating uncharted waters, this journey promises to equip you with the knowledge, inspiration, and tools needed to chart your course in the world of Affiliate Marketing.

Get ready to redefine your understanding, ignite your ambitions, and unleash the potential that Affiliate Marketing holds. The adventure begins now.

What is Affiliate Marketing?

At its core, Affiliate Marketing is a symphony of mutual benefit, orchestrated across the digital realm. It's a symbiotic relationship between individuals and businesses, where each note struck resonates with the promise of prosperity.

Picture this: you're an affiliate, a modern-day matchmaker. You curate a selection of products or services that align with your interests, passions, or expertise. These offerings, handpicked from a range of businesses, become your portfolio. Your goal? To captivate an audience that shares your enthusiasm.

Now, imagine the business side of the stage. Companies with remarkable products seek an audience to dazzle. They're the merchants, ready to partner with affiliates who can amplify their reach. They recognize the power of recommendation — that personal touch that bridges the gap between potential customer and lifelong advocate.

This is where the dance begins. As an affiliate, you weave your portfolio into compelling content — blog posts, videos, social media, whatever suits your style. Your audience, drawn to your authenticity, engages with your content and, intrigued by your recommendations, takes the plunge and purchases.

But here's the magic: behind the scenes, technology tracks this journey. It traces the steps from your content to the merchant's virtual storefront. This tracking isn't just a trail; it's a golden thread that you've woven. When a purchase is made, you're rewarded, not just with the satisfaction of a successful recommendation, but with a slice of the profits. Your efforts are acknowledged and appreciated through commissions.

Affiliate Marketing, in essence, is the art of bridging trust, value, and profit. It's a symphony where everyone — the affiliate, the merchant, and the customer — finds their harmonious note. It's a new-age alliance where entrepreneurship, creativity, and technology converge to create a melody that resonates with the aspirations of modern commerce.

Brief History of Affiliate Marketing

The roots of Affiliate Marketing stretch back to the earliest days of e-commerce, when the internet was still finding its footing. The year was 1989, and a company called PC Flowers & Gifts pioneered what would become the foundation of affiliate programs.

PC Flowers & Gifts launched a program that allowed other websites to link to their online store, and these affiliates would earn a commission for each sale that originated from their referral. This marked the birth of a revolutionary concept: a symbiotic partnership between online businesses and independent marketers, all facilitated by digital connections.

As the 1990s unfolded, Amazon, the e-commerce behemoth, played a pivotal role in shaping the landscape. In 1996, Amazon launched its Associates Program, inviting website owners to advertise and link to Amazon products. This program became a blueprint for modern affiliate marketing, setting the stage for countless partnerships to come.

The early 2000s saw a surge in the number of businesses adopting affiliate programs, as companies recognized the potential of tapping into the vast reach of internet communities. Brands like CDNow, eBay, and others embraced this model, giving rise to the concept of "monetizing" websites.

As technology advanced, tracking and attribution mechanisms evolved, enabling affiliates and merchants to better quantify the impact of their collaborations. Innovations like cookies, which could identify the source of referrals, paved the way for more accurate commission attribution.

The 2010s brought further evolution, with the rise of influencer marketing and content creation. Social media platforms allowed affiliates to engage directly with their audiences, fostering a more personal connection. Affiliate networks, acting as intermediaries, flourished, making it easier for both affiliates and merchants to find suitable partners.

Today, Affiliate Marketing stands as a vibrant and integral part of the digital economy. It's a dynamic ecosystem that has matured from its humble beginnings into a multi-billion-dollar industry. The history of Affiliate Marketing is one of adaptation, innovation, and collaboration, demonstrating the enduring power of partnership in an ever-evolving digital landscape.

Why Affiliate Marketing Matters

Affiliate Marketing matters because it embodies the spirit of collaboration in the digital age, transforming the way businesses grow and individuals prosper. Here's why it holds immense significance:

- Cost-Efficient Growth: For businesses, Affiliate Marketing offers a performance-based model. They only pay when a sale is made, reducing upfront marketing costs and ensuring efficient allocation of resources.
- Expansive Reach: Affiliates come from diverse backgrounds and niches, each with their own audience. This enables businesses to tap into markets they might not have reached otherwise, expanding their customer base.

- Innovation and Creativity: Affiliates bring a fresh perspective to marketing. Their creative content and innovative strategies inject new life into campaigns, resonating with audiences in unique ways.

- Customer-Centric Approach: Affiliates are often trusted figures in their communities. Their recommendations carry weight, fostering a more genuine and trustworthy connection between brands and consumers.

- Empowerment of Individuals: Affiliate Marketing empowers individuals to become entrepreneurs without the traditional business overhead. It opens doors to earning potential for content creators, bloggers, social media influencers, and more.

- Data-Driven Insights: The digital nature of Affiliate Marketing allows for detailed tracking and analytics. This data provides valuable insights into consumer behavior, helping businesses refine their strategies.

- Adaptability: The model is flexible and adaptable to different industries, products, and target audiences. It can work for both physical and digital products, making it a versatile marketing tool.

- Win-Win Dynamics: The essence of Affiliate Marketing is mutual benefit. Businesses grow their sales, affiliates earn commissions, and consumers discover valuable products or services. It's a true win-win-win scenario.

- Global Connectivity: The internet erases geographical boundaries. Affiliates can promote products to a global audience, transcending physical limitations and enabling cross-border partnerships.

- Driving Online Economy: Affiliate Marketing plays a significant role in driving online commerce and contributing to the growth of the digital economy.

In essence, Affiliate Marketing matters because it represents the democratization of marketing, where anyone with passion, creativity, and determination can carve out their niche and thrive. It's a testament to the power of collaboration, innovation, and entrepreneurship in the modern world.

How Affiliate Marketing Works

Affiliate Marketing operates as a dynamic ecosystem of collaboration and profit-sharing. At its core, the process involves three key players: the merchant, the affiliate, and the customer. Here's how it works:

- Merchant (Advertiser): This is the business or company that offers products or services for sale. The merchant seeks to expand its reach and boost sales by partnering with affiliates who can promote their offerings to a wider audience.
- Affiliate (Publisher): Affiliates are independent marketers, content creators, bloggers, influencers, or website owners who have an online presence and an

engaged audience. They join affiliate programs offered by merchants to promote their products or services.

- Customer: The end-consumer who discovers the affiliate's content and decides to purchase the merchant's product or service through the affiliate's referral link.

The Affiliate Marketing process unfolds in a series of steps:

- Affiliate Enrollment: Affiliates sign up for an affiliate program offered by a merchant. This typically involves agreeing to the terms and conditions, and receiving a unique affiliate ID or tracking code.
- Promotion: The affiliate creates compelling content that promotes the merchant's products or services. This

content can take various forms, such as blog posts, videos, social media posts, reviews, and more. The content includes affiliate tracking links, which contain the affiliate's unique ID.

- Audience Engagement: The affiliate shares their content with their audience. This audience could be followers on social media, readers of a blog, viewers of videos, or subscribers to an email list.

- Referral and Tracking: When a member of the audience clicks on the affiliate's tracking link, they are redirected to the merchant's website. The tracking link carries the affiliate's unique ID, allowing the merchant to identify the source of the referral.

- Conversion: If the referred customer makes a purchase on the merchant's website, the tracking system records the transaction and attributes it to the specific affiliate who referred the customer.

- Commission: The affiliate earns a commission on the sale, based on the terms of the affiliate program. Commissions can be a percentage of the sale amount or a fixed fee.
- Tracking and Payments: Affiliate networks or tracking platforms manage the tracking of sales and commission calculations. They ensure accurate attribution and handle the payment process, distributing earnings to affiliates based on the agreed-upon schedule.
- Mutual Growth: As affiliates continue to create valuable content and drive sales, they earn commissions, and the merchant benefits from increased

visibility, brand exposure, and sales growth.

In summary, Affiliate Marketing is a powerful model that harnesses the reach of affiliates, the offerings of merchants, and the purchasing intent of consumers. It's a win-win scenario where everyone involved has the potential to prosper through collaboration and shared success.

The Affiliate Marketing Ecosystem

The Affiliate Marketing ecosystem is a vibrant and interconnected network that thrives on collaboration, innovation, and mutual benefit. At its heart, it consists of several key components:

- Merchants/Advertisers: These are businesses or individuals that offer products or services for sale. They initiate affiliate programs to tap into the promotional power of affiliates and expand their reach to new audiences.
- Affiliates/Publishers: Affiliates are independent marketers who promote products or services through various channels, leveraging their online presence and audience engagement. They drive traffic and potential customers to

the merchant's website using unique tracking links.

- Affiliate Networks/Platforms: These intermediaries connect merchants and affiliates. They provide a platform for merchants to list their affiliate programs and for affiliates to discover and join these programs. Networks also offer tracking tools, reporting, and commission payment facilitation.

- Customers/Consumers: The ultimate beneficiaries of the ecosystem, customers make purchases based on the recommendations of affiliates. They enjoy access to valuable information and products tailored to their interests.

- Tracking and Attribution Systems: Technology plays a pivotal role in Affiliate Marketing. Tracking systems monitor affiliate-referral interactions, ensuring accurate attribution of sales to the appropriate affiliates. Cookies, unique IDs, and tracking links are common tools used to achieve this.

- Content Creation Channels: Affiliates use various platforms to create and share content that promotes the merchant's products. These can include websites, blogs, social media channels, YouTube, podcasts, and email newsletters.

- Promotional Strategies: Affiliates employ diverse strategies to engage their audience and encourage conversions. These can include product reviews, tutorials, comparison articles, influencer endorsements, and limited-time promotions.

- Commission Models: Merchants define the commission structures for their affiliate programs. Commissions can be based on a percentage of the sale amount, a fixed fee per sale, a hybrid of both, or even recurring commissions for subscription-based products.

- Analytics and Reporting: Both merchants and affiliates rely on data to optimize their strategies. Analytics provide insights into traffic sources, conversion rates, and the performance of different marketing channels.

- Regulatory Compliance: As Affiliate Marketing involves endorsements and promotions, it must adhere to legal and ethical standards. This includes transparency in disclosures and compliance with relevant regulations, such as those set by the Federal Trade Commission (FTC).

- Innovation and Technology: The ecosystem continuously evolves with technological advancements. Innovations like deep linking (directing users to specific product pages) and cross-device tracking enhance the user experience and affiliate earnings.

- Global Reach: Affiliate Marketing knows no geographical bounds. Affiliates can connect with merchants from around the world, promoting products to a global audience.

In essence, the Affiliate Marketing ecosystem thrives on the collaborative efforts of merchants, affiliates, and customers, facilitated by technology, creativity, and a shared goal of driving sales and mutual success.

Role of Key Players: Merchants, Affiliates, Customers

Here's a breakdown of the roles of the key players in Affiliate Marketing: Merchants, Affiliates, and Customers.

Merchants/Advertisers:

- Offer Products or Services: Merchants are businesses or individuals who have products or services available for sale. They create affiliate programs to expand their customer base and reach.

- Provide Marketing Resources: Merchants equip affiliates with marketing materials such as banners, product images, and promotional content to help them effectively promote the products.

- Set Commission Structures: Merchants define the commission rates and terms for affiliates. They determine how much affiliates earn for driving sales or leads.

- Manage Affiliate Relationships: Merchants manage their relationships with affiliates, approving or disapproving applications, and addressing any questions or concerns.

Affiliates/Publishers:

- Promote Products: Affiliates create and distribute content to promote the merchant's products or services. This can include reviews, tutorials, blog posts, social media posts, videos, and more.

- Generate Traffic and Leads: Affiliates drive traffic to the merchant's website through their content and referral links. Their goal is to encourage potential customers to make purchases.

- Build Trust and Authority: Affiliates often build a loyal audience by providing valuable content and establishing themselves as trustworthy sources of information in their chosen niche.

- Optimize Campaigns: Affiliates analyze data to refine their strategies. They may experiment with different promotional techniques, audience targeting, and content formats to optimize conversions.

- Earn Commissions: Affiliates earn commissions for each successful referral or sale that they drive. Commissions are a direct result of their efforts and the value they bring to the merchant.

Customers/Consumers:

- Discover Recommendations: Customers come across affiliate-created content that resonates with their interests or needs. This content introduces them to products or services they might not have discovered otherwise.

- Engage with Content: Customers engage with the affiliate's content, gaining insights, information, and recommendations about the products.
- Make Purchases: If convinced by the affiliate's content, customers click on the affiliate's referral link and make purchases on the merchant's website.
- Enjoy Benefits: Customers benefit from the products or services they purchase. They may also enjoy special discounts or offers that affiliates provide.
- Support Affiliates: By making purchases through affiliate links, customers support the affiliates whose recommendations they value.

In this dynamic ecosystem, merchants benefit from increased sales, affiliates earn commissions for their efforts, and customers gain access to products that align with their interests or needs. The success of Affiliate Marketing relies on the harmonious interaction and collaboration of these key players.

Tracking and Attribution Mechanisms

In the labyrinthine world of Affiliate Marketing, tracking and attribution mechanisms act as the guiding stars, illuminating the path from a potential customer's first interaction to a successful sale. These mechanisms form the cornerstone of trust, transparency, and fair compensation within the ecosystem.

1. Tracking Links and Unique IDs:

At the heart of tracking lies the humble tracking link. When an affiliate creates content to promote a product, they embed a special tracking link that contains a unique affiliate ID. This link acts as a digital fingerprint, allowing the merchant to trace the customer's journey back to the affiliate who initiated it.

2. Cookies and Browser Tracking:

Cookies are the virtual breadcrumbs of the internet. When a user clicks on an affiliate's tracking link, a cookie is placed on their device. This cookie holds information about the affiliate's ID and the referring link. Even if the user navigates away from the site and returns later to make a purchase, the cookie ensures the sale is attributed to the correct affiliate.

3. Cross-Device Tracking:

In today's multi-device landscape, users might explore a product on their phone, research it on their laptop, and finally make the purchase on their tablet. Cross-device tracking ensures that the affiliate receives credit regardless of the device used to make the purchase.

4. First-Click and Last-Click Attribution:

Two common attribution models are "first-click" and "last-click." In the first-click model, the affiliate who introduced the customer to the product receives the commission, regardless of subsequent interactions. In the last-click model, the affiliate whose link the customer clicked last before making the purchase gets the commission.

5. Multi-Touch Attribution:

Recognizing that customer journeys are rarely linear, multi-touch attribution models assign value to each touchpoint along the way. This more accurately reflects the contributions of different affiliates or marketing channels in the customer's decision-making process.

6. Attribution Windows:

An attribution window defines the timeframe during which a sale must occur for the affiliate to receive credit. Common windows include "last-click wins" (within a short period after clicking) or "view-through" (where affiliates receive credit even if the customer didn't click the link but saw the content).

7. Affiliate Networks and Tracking Platforms:

Affiliate networks and tracking platforms provide the technology to manage these mechanisms. They offer tools to generate tracking links, monitor clicks, record conversions, and calculate commissions. These platforms ensure fairness and accuracy in the attribution process.

In essence, tracking and attribution mechanisms are the invisible architects of

Affiliate Marketing. They ensure that the efforts of affiliates are rightfully acknowledged, creating a system where every click, interaction, and purchase has a traceable path, fostering transparency, trust, and a thriving ecosystem of collaboration.

Getting Started as an Affiliate

Embarking on the journey of becoming an affiliate is like setting sail into uncharted waters with a treasure map in hand. It's an exciting endeavor that requires careful planning, enthusiasm, and a touch of strategic finesse. Here's how to navigate the seas of Affiliate Marketing as you get started:

1. Define Your Niche:

Select a niche that aligns with your interests, expertise, and the preferences of your target audience. This specialization not only makes your content more authentic but also helps you connect with a dedicated audience.

2. Research Affiliate Programs:

Explore affiliate programs that match your chosen niche. Look for programs that offer products or services your audience would find valuable. Research the commission structures, payment methods, and terms of each program.

3. Choose Quality Products:

Opt for products or services that resonate with your values and genuinely benefit your audience. Promoting quality offerings builds trust with your audience and ensures that your recommendations hold weight.

4. Build Your Online Presence:

Create a platform for your affiliate efforts. This could be a blog, website, YouTube channel, podcast, or social media profiles. Your platform serves as the stage for your content and the bridge between your audience and the products you promote.

5. Develop High-Quality Content:
Craft content that adds value to your audience's lives. This could include product reviews, tutorials, how-to guides, comparisons, or engaging storytelling. Your content should be informative, engaging, and relevant to your niche.

6. Utilize Multiple Channels:
Diversify your content distribution by using various channels. Don't limit yourself to just one platform; leverage social media, email marketing, video content, and written content to reach a broader audience.

7. Incorporate Affiliate Links:

Integrate your affiliate links naturally into your content. Ensure that they blend seamlessly with your recommendations and don't come across as overly promotional.

8. Focus on Audience Engagement:
Build a genuine connection with your audience. Engage with their comments, respond to questions, and listen to their feedback. This interaction cultivates a community around your niche.

9. Monitor and Optimize:
Regularly analyze the performance of your content. Pay attention to metrics such as click-through rates, conversion rates, and earnings. Use this data to refine your strategies and create more effective content.

10. Stay Ethical and Transparent:

Disclose your affiliate relationships to your audience. Transparency fosters trust and ensures that your audience knows when you're promoting products for which you may receive compensation.

11. Be Patient and Persistent:

Success in affiliate marketing takes time. Be patient and persistent as you grow your audience, refine your strategies, and build a reputation as a credible affiliate marketer.

Remember, getting started as an affiliate is just the first step. With dedication, continuous learning, and a commitment to delivering value, you can set sail on a journey that holds the promise of meaningful connections, financial reward, and the satisfaction of helping your audience discover valuable products.

Finding a Profitable Niche

In the vast landscape of Affiliate Marketing, finding a profitable niche is like discovering a hidden treasure chest. A well-chosen niche not only helps you stand out amidst the digital noise but also lays the foundation for a sustainable and rewarding affiliate journey. Here's how to embark on the quest of finding your profitable niche:

1. Self-Reflection and Passion:
Start by examining your own passions, interests, and areas of expertise. Consider what topics genuinely excite you and ignite your curiosity. Your enthusiasm will naturally translate into authentic content that resonates with your audience.

2. Research Market Demand:

While passion is crucial, it's equally important to assess the demand for your chosen niche. Research keywords, trends, and search volumes to gauge whether people are actively seeking information related to your niche.

3. Audience Identification:

Define your target audience within the chosen niche. Understand their needs, problems, and preferences. The more accurately you can pinpoint your audience's characteristics, the better you can tailor your content to their interests.

4. Competition Analysis:

Analyze the competition within your chosen niche. Are there established affiliates or businesses already catering to this audience? While competition is a sign of demand, consider how you can differentiate yourself by bringing a unique perspective or value proposition.

5. Profitability and Monetization:
Assess the monetization potential of the niche. Research affiliate programs, products, and services that are available for promotion within your niche. Are there products that offer attractive commissions and align with your audience's needs?

6. Longevity and Trends:
Consider the long-term sustainability of the niche. Is it a passing trend or a topic that will remain relevant over time? Aim for a niche with evergreen qualities to ensure your efforts continue to yield results.

7. Problem Solving:

Niche selection often boils down to addressing problems or fulfilling needs. Identify pain points or gaps in your chosen niche and position yourself as a solution provider through your content and affiliate recommendations.

8. Blend of Passion and Profit:
Ideally, your chosen niche should be a harmonious blend of your passion and profit potential. While profitability is essential, genuine interest in the topic will keep you motivated and engaged in the long run.

9. Test and Iterate:
Niche selection doesn't have to be set in stone. It's okay to test the waters with different niches and see which ones resonate most with your audience. Be willing to pivot if you discover a more promising direction.

10. Stay Open to Evolution:

Remember that niches can evolve and change over time. As you gain insights and learn more about your audience, you might uncover new subtopics or areas to explore within your niche.

In the grand tapestry of Affiliate Marketing, your chosen niche is the vibrant thread that weaves through your content and connects you with your audience. By blending your passions, market demand, and a strategic approach, you can uncover a profitable niche that not only rewards you financially but also fulfills your creative aspirations.

Choosing the Right Affiliate Programs

Selecting the right affiliate programs is akin to assembling a puzzle where each piece contributes to the bigger picture of your success. The affiliate programs you choose to partner with will shape the products you promote, the commissions you earn, and the overall direction of your affiliate journey. Here's how to navigate the landscape and choose the right programs:

1. Alignment with Your Niche:
Ensure that the affiliate programs you choose align closely with your chosen niche. The products or services should resonate with your audience's interests and needs, creating a seamless connection between your content and the recommendations you make.

2. Product Quality and Reputation:

Promote products that you can vouch for. Quality matters. If you're endorsing subpar products, your credibility could be compromised. Choose programs associated with reputable brands that offer value to your audience.

3. Commission Structure:

Examine the commission rates offered by different affiliate programs. While higher commissions are enticing, also consider the product's price point and conversion potential. Sometimes a moderate commission on a high-priced product can yield significant earnings.

4. Cookie Duration:

Look into the cookie duration offered by affiliate programs. A longer cookie duration means you'll receive credit for conversions that occur even if they happen days or weeks after the initial click.

5. Conversion Rates and Earnings Potential:
Research the historical conversion rates of the affiliate program. High conversion rates indicate that the product is well-received by customers. Combine this information with the commission structure to estimate your potential earnings.

6. Affiliate Support and Resources:
Evaluate the support and resources provided by the affiliate program. This can include marketing materials, banners, product information, and dedicated affiliate managers who can assist you in your promotional efforts.

7. Payment Method and Frequency:

Check the payment methods and frequency of payouts. Some programs offer monthly payouts, while others might have a minimum earnings threshold that needs to be reached before payments are processed.

8. Tracking and Reporting:
Choose programs that offer robust tracking and reporting capabilities. Accurate data on clicks, conversions, and earnings is essential for optimizing your strategies and understanding what's working best.

9. Program Reputation and Reviews:
Search for reviews and testimonials from other affiliates who have worked with the program. Their experiences can provide insights into the program's reliability, communication, and overall affiliate satisfaction.

10. Ethical Considerations:

Ensure that the products you're promoting align with your ethical values. Avoid promoting products that could potentially harm your audience or compromise their trust in you.

11. Diversity of Products:

Consider programs that offer a variety of products or a product catalog that complements your niche. This diversity can provide you with more options to cater to your audience's preferences.

12. Long-Term Viability:

Choose affiliate programs that have a long-term outlook. Programs that have been around for a while and show commitment to their affiliates are more likely to provide stable opportunities.

By carefully evaluating these factors, you can select affiliate programs that not only offer lucrative earning potential but also resonate with your audience and support your long-term goals as an affiliate marketer.

Setting Up Your Online Presence

Setting up your online presence is like constructing the stage upon which your affiliate marketing journey unfolds. It's the digital canvas where you'll paint your content, connect with your audience, and showcase the products you promote. Here's how to lay a strong foundation for your online presence:

1. Choose a Platform:
Select the platform that best suits your content style and audience preferences. This could be a blog, website, YouTube channel, podcast, or a combination of these. The platform you choose will be your home base for creating and sharing content.

2. Secure a Domain and Hosting:

If you're setting up a blog or website, secure a domain name that reflects your niche or brand. Choose a reliable hosting service that ensures your website is accessible and loads quickly for visitors.

3. Design and Branding:
Design your online presence with a cohesive and appealing visual identity. Choose colors, fonts, and graphics that resonate with your niche and create a memorable brand image. Consistency in design builds recognition.

4. Create Essential Pages:
Craft important pages that provide essential information to your visitors. These might include an "About Me" page that introduces yourself, a "Contact" page for audience interaction, and a "Disclosure" page explaining your affiliate relationships.

5. Develop High-Quality Content:

Start creating high-quality content that aligns with your chosen niche. Ensure your content provides value, educates, entertains, or solves problems for your target audience. High-quality content is the cornerstone of a successful online presence.

6. Incorporate SEO Strategies:

Implement search engine optimization (SEO) techniques to make your content discoverable by search engines. Use relevant keywords, optimize meta descriptions, and ensure your content is structured for readability.

7. Content Calendar:

Create a content calendar to plan and organize your content creation. Consistency is key, so establish a posting schedule that you can realistically maintain.

8. Social Media Presence:

Set up social media profiles on platforms that align with your audience. Share your content, engage with your followers, and use social media as an extension of your online presence.

9. Optimize for Mobile:

Ensure your online presence is mobile-friendly. With a significant portion of internet users accessing content on mobile devices, a responsive design is essential for a seamless user experience.

10. Collect Audience Data:

Implement tools to collect audience data, such as email sign-up forms. Building an email list allows you to maintain direct communication with your audience and promote your content and affiliate offers.

11. Interact and Engage:

Engage with your audience by responding to comments, questions, and feedback. Create a sense of community by fostering discussions and connections among your audience members.

12. Stay Current and Evolve:

Regularly update your content and adapt to changes in your niche and the online landscape. Embrace new tools, trends, and technologies to keep your online presence fresh and relevant.

Setting up your online presence is an investment in your affiliate marketing success. It's the virtual realm where you'll build relationships, share insights, and create a space that draws your audience in and keeps them coming back for more.

Creating High-Converting Content

Creating high-converting content is the art of crafting a compelling narrative that not only captivates your audience but also drives them to take action. It's about turning casual readers into engaged followers and potential customers. Here's how to master the craft of creating content that converts:

1. Understand Your Audience:
Know your audience inside out. Understand their needs, pain points, aspirations, and preferences. Tailor your content to resonate with them on a personal level.

2. Start with a Strong Hook:
Capture your audience's attention from the very beginning. Use intriguing headlines, compelling

introductions, and relatable anecdotes to draw readers in.

3. Provide Value and Solutions:
Your content should offer real value to your audience. Address their problems, answer their questions, and provide actionable solutions. The more you help them, the more likely they are to trust your recommendations.

4. Craft Engaging Storytelling:
Tell stories that resonate emotionally. Stories create a connection with your audience and make your content more memorable. Share personal experiences, success stories, and relatable scenarios.

5. Utilize Visuals:
Incorporate visuals such as images, infographics, and videos to enhance your

content. Visual elements break up text and make your content more engaging and digestible.

6. Use Clear and Compelling Language:
Write in a clear and concise manner. Avoid jargon or overly technical terms that might confuse your audience. Use language that resonates with your readers and communicates your points effectively.

7. Highlight Benefits:
Focus on the benefits of the products or services you're promoting. How will they solve problems, improve lives, or enhance experiences? Clearly articulate these benefits to your audience.

8. Include Social Proof:

Incorporate social proof such as customer reviews, testimonials, or case studies. Social proof adds credibility and demonstrates that others have benefited from the products you're promoting.

9. Create a Call to Action (CTA):
Guide your readers on the next step to take. Whether it's clicking an affiliate link, signing up for a newsletter, or making a purchase, a clear and persuasive CTA encourages action.

10. Establish Authority:
Position yourself as an authority in your niche. Back up your content with research, data, and expertise. When your audience sees you as knowledgeable, they're more likely to trust your recommendations.

11. Build Trust Through Transparency:

Be transparent about your affiliate relationships. Disclose your affiliations and explain why you're recommending certain products. Trust is essential for converting readers into customers.

12. Test and Optimize:
Experiment with different content formats and approaches. Use analytics to track the performance of your content. Learn from what works and refine your strategies for even better results.

Creating high-converting content is a blend of creativity, strategy, and understanding your audience's needs. By delivering value, building trust, and guiding your readers towards action, you can transform your content into a powerful tool for driving conversions and achieving affiliate marketing success.

Crafting Compelling Product Reviews

Crafting compelling product reviews is an art that requires a balance of informative content and persuasive storytelling. A well-written review can be a powerful tool for guiding your audience's purchasing decisions and boosting your affiliate commissions. Here's how to create product reviews that captivate and convert:

1. Experience the Product:

Before you review a product, use it yourself. This firsthand experience allows you to provide genuine insights and details that resonate with your audience.

2. Start with an Engaging Introduction:

Capture your readers' attention right from the beginning. Share a relatable scenario, an interesting fact, or a problem the product solves. Your introduction sets the tone for the rest of the review.

3. Provide Detailed Information:
Offer comprehensive information about the product's features, benefits, and specifications. Describe how the product works, what sets it apart, and how it addresses your audience's needs.

4. Share Personal Experiences:
Integrate personal anecdotes and experiences with the product. Describe how the product has impacted your life, solved a problem, or improved your routine. Personal stories humanize your review and make it relatable.

5. Highlight Pros and Cons:
Provide a balanced perspective by discussing both the positives and potential drawbacks of

the product. This demonstrates honesty and credibility, making your review more trustworthy.

6. Use Visuals:

Include high-quality images and even videos of the product. Visuals help your audience get a clear understanding of the product's appearance and functionality.

7. Compare and Contrast:

If applicable, compare the product with similar alternatives. Highlight what makes this product stand out and how it fares in comparison. This helps readers make informed choices.

8. Address Common Concerns:

Anticipate and address potential questions or concerns your audience might have. Providing solutions to common doubts can alleviate hesitations and encourage conversions.

9. Incorporate Social Proof:

Include customer reviews, testimonials, or user-generated content related to the product. Social proof reinforces your review and adds credibility.

10. Offer Practical Use Cases:

Demonstrate how the product can be used in real-life scenarios. Paint a vivid picture of how it fits into your audience's daily routine and solves their problems.

11. Share Data and Statistics:

If applicable, use data and statistics to back up your claims. Numbers lend credibility and help readers understand the product's impact more tangibly.

12. Conclude with a Strong Call to Action:
Wrap up your review by encouraging your readers to take action. Include a clear call to action that guides them to the next steps, whether it's visiting the product's website or making a purchase.

Crafting compelling product reviews requires a blend of authenticity, information, and persuasion. When your review resonates with your audience, addresses their concerns, and guides them toward making a decision, you create a valuable resource that not only informs but also influences purchasing choices.

Producing Informative Tutorials and Guides

Producing informative tutorials and guides is like handing your audience a treasure map that leads them through the maze of knowledge and skills they're seeking. Well-crafted tutorials and guides not only position you as an expert but also provide immense value to your audience. Here's how to create content that educates, empowers, and engages:

1. Choose Relevant Topics:
Select topics that align with your niche and address your audience's needs. Consider common pain points, questions, and challenges they might have.

2. Break Down Complex Concepts:
Tutorials and guides are opportunities to simplify complex ideas. Break down

information into manageable steps, and use clear language to ensure your audience can easily follow along.

3. Establish a Clear Structure:
Organize your content with a logical flow. Use headings, subheadings, and bullet points to make it easy for readers to navigate and absorb the information.

4. Use Visuals and Examples:
Incorporate visuals such as images, diagrams, infographics, and screenshots to enhance understanding. Examples and case studies add context and practicality to your content.

5. Step-by-Step Instructions:
Provide detailed, step-by-step instructions for each task or concept. Clearly outline what needs to be done, how to do it, and why it's important.

6. Anticipate Questions:

While creating your tutorial, think about the questions your audience might have at each step. Address these questions preemptively to avoid confusion.

7. Be Thorough but Concise:

Deliver thorough explanations without overwhelming your audience. Be concise in your writing, getting to the point while covering all essential information.

8. Include Actionable Tips:

Share tips, shortcuts, and best practices that can enhance the reader's experience. Offering practical insights adds value and encourages engagement.

9. Provide Solutions to Problems:

Focus on solving specific problems or challenges your audience faces. Your tutorials should offer solutions that help them overcome obstacles.

10. Interactive Elements:
Incorporate interactive elements like quizzes, interactive checklists, or downloadable resources that readers can use to reinforce their learning.

11. Encourage Hands-On Learning:
Whenever possible, encourage readers to apply what they've learned. Include exercises or tasks that allow them to practice and solidify their understanding.

12. Call to Action:
Conclude your tutorial or guide with a call to action that encourages readers to take the next

steps. This could be exploring related content, subscribing to your newsletter, or exploring affiliate products.

By producing informative tutorials and guides, you're not only sharing valuable knowledge but also positioning yourself as a trusted resource in your niche. As you help your audience master new skills, overcome challenges, and achieve their goals, you establish a connection that keeps them coming back for more of your valuable content.

Optimizing Your Website for Conversions

Optimizing your website for conversions is the art of creating a digital environment that encourages visitors to take specific actions, whether it's making a purchase, signing up for a newsletter, or clicking on an affiliate link. Here's how to transform your website into a conversion powerhouse:

1. Clear and Intuitive Design:
Simplicity is key. Your website's design should be clean, easy to navigate, and intuitive. Use a logical layout that guides visitors seamlessly from one section to another.

2. Mobile-Friendly Design:
Ensure your website is responsive and looks great on various devices, including smartphones and tablets. A mobile-friendly

design enhances user experience and accommodates different browsing habits.

3. Speed and Performance:
A fast-loading website is crucial for retaining visitors. Optimize images, use browser caching, and choose a reliable hosting service to ensure your website loads quickly.

4. Compelling Call to Action (CTA):
Place clear and persuasive CTAs strategically throughout your website. Use actionable language and vibrant colors to attract attention and prompt action.

5. Relevant and High-Quality Content:
Content that resonates with your audience keeps them engaged and encourages them to explore further. Deliver valuable information that aligns with their interests and needs.

6. Visual Hierarchy:

Utilize visual hierarchy to guide visitors' attention. Highlight important elements like CTAs, headings, and key information using size, color, and placement.

7. Optimize Landing Pages:

If you're running specific campaigns, create dedicated landing pages. These pages should be tailored to the campaign's message and have a clear focus on the desired action.

8. A/B Testing:

Experiment with different variations of elements such as headlines, CTAs, and colors. A/B testing helps you identify what resonates best with your audience and boosts conversion rates.

9. Reduce Friction:

Minimize obstacles that might deter visitors from taking action. Simplify forms, reduce the number of steps required, and make the checkout process smooth.

10. Social Proof:

Incorporate testimonials, reviews, and user-generated content to demonstrate that others have benefited from your content or affiliate products. Social proof builds credibility.

11. Exit-Intent Popups:

Use exit-intent popups to capture visitors who are about to leave your website. Offer incentives such as discounts, free resources, or newsletters to entice them to stay or take action.

12. Analyze and Iterate:

Regularly review website analytics to gain insights into user behavior. Identify bottlenecks, drop-off points, and areas of improvement. Use this data to refine your strategies.

Optimizing your website for conversions involves creating a seamless user experience that guides visitors towards the desired outcomes. By strategically designing your website, offering valuable content, and fine-tuning elements based on data, you can transform your website into a conversion engine that maximizes your affiliate marketing success.

Strategies for Effective Promotion

Effective promotion is the heartbeat of successful affiliate marketing. It's about reaching your target audience, engaging them, and encouraging them to take action on the products or services you're promoting. Here are strategies to amplify your promotion efforts:

1. Content Marketing:
Create high-quality content that educates, entertains, or solves problems for your audience. This could include blog posts, articles, videos, podcasts, and infographics. Integrate your affiliate links naturally within your content.

2. SEO Optimization:

Optimize your content for search engines. Use relevant keywords, meta descriptions, and headings to ensure your content ranks well in search results and reaches a wider audience.

3. Social Media Marketing:
Leverage social media platforms to connect with your audience. Share your content, engage in discussions, and build a community around your niche. Use eye-catching visuals and interactive elements to capture attention.

4. Email Marketing:
Build an email list and send regular newsletters to your subscribers. Share valuable content, product recommendations, and exclusive offers. Email marketing allows you to maintain direct communication with your audience.

5. Influencer Partnerships:

Collaborate with influencers or bloggers in your niche. Influencers can introduce your affiliate products to their established audience, lending credibility and trust to your recommendations.

6. Video Marketing:

Create video content on platforms like YouTube or social media. Video tutorials, reviews, and demonstrations are effective ways to engage and educate your audience about the products you're promoting.

7. Webinars and Live Streams:

Host webinars or live streams where you discuss relevant topics and demonstrate the value of the products. Interact with your audience in real time and address their questions.

8. Guest Posting:

Write guest posts for reputable websites in your niche. This exposes your content and affiliate links to a new audience while establishing your authority in the field.

9. Affiliate Giveaways and Contests:
Organize giveaways or contests that require participants to engage with your content or products. This generates buzz, increases engagement, and expands your reach.

10. Paid Advertising:
Consider using paid advertising such as Google Ads, social media ads, or native advertising. Paid ads can drive targeted traffic to your content and affiliate links.

11. Cross-Promotion:
Collaborate with fellow affiliates or content creators to cross-promote each other's content

or products. This expands your reach to new audiences.

12. Webinars and Live Streams:
Host webinars or live streams where you discuss relevant topics and demonstrate the value of the products. Interact with your audience in real time and address their questions.

Remember that effective promotion is a dynamic process that requires continuous refinement. Monitor the performance of your strategies using analytics, gather feedback from your audience, and adapt your approach based on what resonates best with them. By using a combination of these strategies, you can create a multi-faceted promotional approach that drives engagement, conversions, and affiliate success.

Leveraging SEO for Affiliate Marketing

Leveraging SEO (Search Engine Optimization) is a strategic approach that can significantly boost your affiliate marketing efforts. By optimizing your content for search engines, you can increase your visibility, attract targeted organic traffic, and enhance the potential for conversions. Here's how to effectively use SEO for affiliate marketing:

1. Keyword Research:
Identify relevant keywords and phrases that your target audience is searching for. Use keyword research tools to find high-volume, low-competition keywords related to the products you're promoting.

2. Quality Content Creation:

Create high-quality, valuable content that addresses the needs and interests of your audience. This could include product reviews, tutorials, guides, and informative articles.

3. On-Page Optimization:
Optimize your content for on-page SEO. Use target keywords in your title, headings, meta descriptions, and throughout the content. However, ensure that keyword usage feels natural and not forced.

4. Engaging Headlines:
Craft compelling headlines that include your target keywords. A well-crafted headline not only captures readers' attention but also improves click-through rates in search results.

5. Internal and External Linking:

Incorporate internal links that connect to other relevant pages on your website. Also, include external links to authoritative sources that provide additional value to your audience.

6. User-Friendly URLs:
Create user-friendly URLs that include your target keywords and succinctly describe the content of the page.

7. Mobile-Friendly Design:
Ensure your website is responsive and mobile-friendly. Google prioritizes mobile-friendly sites in search rankings.

8. Page Loading Speed:
Optimize your website's loading speed by compressing images, leveraging browser caching, and choosing a reliable hosting service.

9. Image Optimization:

Optimize images by using descriptive filenames and alt tags. This not only helps with SEO but also improves accessibility.

10. Publish Consistently:

Consistency matters in SEO. Regularly publish new content to keep your website active and attract search engine crawlers.

11. Monitor Analytics:

Use tools like Google Analytics to monitor your website's performance. Analyze metrics such as traffic, bounce rate, and conversion rates to identify areas for improvement.

12. Build Quality Backlinks:

Earn backlinks from reputable websites in your niche. High-quality backlinks signal to search engines that your content is trustworthy and valuable.

13. Long-Form Content:
Incorporate long-form content that thoroughly covers topics related to the products you're promoting. Google tends to favor comprehensive and authoritative content.

14. Focus on User Experience:
Prioritize user experience by creating intuitive navigation, improving readability, and ensuring that your website is easy to navigate and explore.

By implementing these SEO strategies, you can enhance your website's visibility in search results and attract a consistent stream of organic traffic. Over time, this can lead to increased affiliate conversions and a stronger online presence within your niche.

Social Media Marketing Techniques

Social media marketing is a dynamic way to engage with your audience, promote affiliate products, and build a loyal community. Here are effective techniques to leverage social media for your affiliate marketing efforts:

1. Choose the Right Platforms:
Identify the social media platforms where your target audience is most active. Whether it's Instagram, Facebook, Twitter, LinkedIn, or others, focus your efforts where your audience spends their time.

2. Consistent Branding:
Maintain consistent branding across your social media profiles. Use the same profile picture, cover photo, and bio to create a recognizable identity.

3. Content Variety:

Share a mix of content types, including product reviews, tutorials, behind-the-scenes glimpses, industry news, and user-generated content. Diversify your content to keep your audience engaged.

4. Visual Content:

Use visuals that grab attention. High-quality images, graphics, videos, and infographics can help convey your messages more effectively.

5. Hashtags Strategically:

Research and use relevant hashtags to increase the visibility of your posts. However, avoid overloading your posts with hashtags; focus on quality over quantity.

6. Engage with Your Audience:

Interact with your followers by responding to comments, asking questions, and starting conversations. Engagement fosters a sense of community and connection.

7. Storytelling:
Share personal stories related to your niche. Stories make your content relatable and help build an emotional connection with your audience.

8. Live Videos and Webinars:
Host live videos or webinars to discuss topics related to your niche and affiliate products. Live sessions allow direct interaction and engagement with your audience.

9. User-Generated Content:
Encourage your followers to create content related to your niche or products. Repost

user-generated content to show appreciation and build a sense of community.

10. Promote Value:
Focus on providing value to your audience. Share tips, insights, and helpful information that align with their interests and needs.

11. Affiliate Link Placement:
Incorporate affiliate links naturally in your content. Avoid being overly promotional; instead, weave them into your posts in a way that adds value to your followers.

12. Collaborations and Partnerships:
Collaborate with influencers, brands, or other affiliates in your niche. Partnerships can help you reach new audiences and increase your credibility.

13. Analyze and Adjust:

Use social media analytics to track the performance of your posts. Identify which content resonates most with your audience and adjust your strategy accordingly.

14. Schedule Posts:

Use scheduling tools to plan and schedule your social media posts in advance. Consistency is key, and scheduling can help you maintain a steady presence.

Social media marketing is an ongoing process that requires adaptability and engagement. By building a strong online presence, providing value, and nurturing relationships with your audience, you can create a thriving social media strategy that supports your affiliate marketing goals.

Email Marketing Campaigns

Email marketing campaigns are a powerful way to directly communicate with your audience, nurture relationships, and promote affiliate products. Here's a step-by-step guide on how to create effective email marketing campaigns for your affiliate marketing efforts:

1. Build Your Email List:
Start by collecting email addresses from interested individuals. Offer incentives such as free guides, ebooks, or exclusive content to encourage sign-ups.

2. Choose an Email Marketing Platform:
Select a reputable email marketing platform that suits your needs. Popular options include Mailchimp, ConvertKit, and AWeber.

3. Segment Your List:

Segment your email list based on factors such as demographics, interests, and engagement levels. This allows you to send targeted and relevant content.

4. Define Campaign Objectives:

Determine the goals of your email campaign. Are you promoting a specific product, sharing valuable content, or announcing a special offer?

5. Craft Compelling Subject Lines:

Write subject lines that grab attention and entice recipients to open your emails. Keep them concise, relevant, and curiosity-inducing.

6. Create Valuable Content:

Develop content that provides value to your subscribers. This could include product recommendations, educational content, tips, or exclusive offers.

7. Incorporate Visuals:

Use images, graphics, and even videos to enhance your email content. Visuals break up text and make your emails more engaging.

8. Personalization:

Address recipients by their first name and tailor your content to their interests. Personalization can significantly increase engagement.

9. Call to Action (CTA):

Include a clear and compelling call to action in your emails. Whether it's clicking an affiliate link, visiting a website, or making a purchase, guide recipients on the desired action.

10. Affiliate Links Placement:

Incorporate affiliate links naturally within your email content. Be transparent about your affiliate relationships to maintain trust.

11. Mobile Optimization:
Ensure your emails are mobile-responsive. Many recipients access emails on their smartphones, so a mobile-friendly design is crucial.

12. Test Before Sending:
Preview and test your emails before sending them to your entire list. Check for formatting issues, broken links, and how the email looks on different devices.

13. Send at Optimal Times:
Send emails at times when your audience is most likely to check their inboxes. Consider

experimenting with different sending times to find what works best for your audience.

14. Monitor and Analyze:
Track the performance of your email campaigns. Monitor open rates, click-through rates, and conversion rates. Use this data to refine your future campaigns.

15. Provide Unsubscribe Option:
Include an easy and clear way for recipients to unsubscribe from your emails. This maintains respect for their preferences and helps you maintain a clean and engaged list.

Email marketing campaigns allow you to build a direct line of communication with your audience and nurture ongoing relationships. By providing valuable content, promoting relevant affiliate products, and tailoring your messages to your subscribers' needs, you can create effective email campaigns that drive engagement and conversions.

Maximizing Affiliate Revenue

Maximizing affiliate revenue requires a strategic approach that combines effective promotion, relationship building, and continuous optimization. Here are strategies to help you make the most of your affiliate marketing efforts:

1. Choose the Right Products:
Select products or services that align with your niche and resonate with your audience's interests and needs. Quality and relevance are key to driving conversions.

2. Understand Your Audience:
Know your audience's pain points, desires, and preferences. Tailor your content and

recommendations to address their specific needs.

3. Build Trust and Credibility:
Establish yourself as a trusted authority in your niche. Provide honest and valuable information, disclose your affiliate relationships, and prioritize your audience's best interests.

4. High-Quality Content:
Create content that delivers value, educates, entertains, or solves problems. High-quality content positions you as a reliable resource and encourages engagement.

5. Diversify Promotion Channels:
Use a variety of promotion channels such as blogs, social media, email marketing, videos,

and podcasts. Diversification increases your reach and exposure.

6. Test and Optimize:
Experiment with different strategies, content formats, and promotional techniques. Monitor the performance of your efforts and refine your approach based on data.

7. Strategic Affiliate Link Placement:
Place affiliate links strategically within your content. Ensure they blend seamlessly and provide context that explains the value of the product to your audience.

8. Monitor Analytics:
Use analytics tools to track your website's performance, conversion rates, and traffic sources. Analyze the data to identify patterns and opportunities.

9. Provide Value Above All:

Prioritize delivering value to your audience. When you genuinely help your readers, they're more likely to trust your recommendations and convert.

10. Build an Email List:

Develop an email list and nurture relationships with your subscribers. Email marketing allows you to maintain direct communication and promote relevant offers.

11. Focus on Long-Term Relationships:

Think beyond short-term gains. Focus on building long-term relationships with your audience. Repeat conversions and loyal customers can lead to sustainable revenue.

12. Stay Updated and Adapt:

Keep up with industry trends, changes in your niche, and new affiliate opportunities. Be willing to adapt your strategies to stay relevant.

13. Leverage Upsells and Cross-Sells:
Promote products that complement the affiliate products you're already promoting. Upselling and cross-selling can increase the average transaction value.

14. Negotiate Higher Commissions:
If you've established a successful track record, consider negotiating higher commission rates with affiliate partners. Your performance can leverage better terms.

15. Continuous Learning:
Stay curious and continue learning about affiliate marketing strategies, SEO techniques,

and content creation. The more you know, the better you can refine your approach.

Remember that maximizing affiliate revenue takes time and effort. Consistency, quality, and a deep understanding of your audience are the cornerstones of building a sustainable and profitable affiliate marketing business.

Understanding Commission Structures

Understanding commission structures is crucial for effectively navigating the world of affiliate marketing and maximizing your earnings. Commission structures define how you'll be compensated for each sale, lead, or action generated through your affiliate links. Here are common types of commission structures:

1. Pay-Per-Sale (PPS) or Cost-Per-Sale (CPS):
In this structure, you earn a fixed percentage or a set amount of commission for each sale made through your affiliate link. This is one of the most common commission models.

2. Pay-Per-Lead (PPL) or Cost-Per-Lead (CPL):
With PPL or CPL, you earn a commission for every lead you refer to the affiliate partner. This

could involve sign-ups for newsletters, trial offers, or other actions that indicate interest.

3. Pay-Per-Click (PPC):
PPC commissions are earned based on the number of clicks your affiliate links receive, regardless of whether those clicks result in sales or leads. This model is less common but still used in some niches.

4. Pay-Per-Action (PPA) or Cost-Per-Action (CPA):
This model encompasses various actions beyond sales or leads, such as downloads, app installations, or form submissions. You receive a commission when a specific action is completed.

5. Tiered Commission Structures:

Some affiliate programs offer tiered commissions, where your earnings increase as you refer more customers or generate higher sales volumes. This rewards affiliates for their performance.

6. Recurring Commissions:
In recurring commission structures, you earn commissions not only for the initial sale but also for ongoing subscriptions or renewals. This model can provide steady income over time.

7. Two-Tier Commissions:
With two-tier commissions, you earn a commission not only for your direct referrals but also for the referrals made by affiliates you've recruited into the program.

8. Exclusive or Custom Agreements:

In certain cases, you might negotiate a unique commission structure directly with the affiliate partner. This could involve hybrid models or tailored terms based on your performance.

9. Cookie Duration:
Consider the cookie duration associated with the affiliate program. Cookies track users who click on your links. A longer cookie duration gives you more time to earn commissions on subsequent purchases.

10. Attribution Models:
Some affiliate programs use attribution models to credit commissions. These models determine which affiliate receives credit if multiple affiliates are involved in a sale or lead.

It's essential to thoroughly understand the commission structure of each affiliate program you join. Factors like the product's price, the type of commission, and the conversion rate can impact your earnings. As you explore different programs, choose those that align with your audience's preferences and have commission structures that reward your efforts effectively.

Scaling Your Affiliate Business

Scaling your affiliate business involves expanding your efforts to reach a larger audience, increase revenue, and enhance your overall impact. Here's a roadmap to help you effectively scale your affiliate marketing business:

1. Optimize Current Strategies:
Before expanding, ensure your current strategies are working efficiently. Analyze your best-performing content, promotion channels, and affiliate products. Refine what's already successful.

2. Expand Content Creation:
Increase the frequency and diversity of your content. Produce more high-quality blog posts,

videos, podcasts, and other forms of content to attract a broader audience.

3. Explore New Niches or Products:
Consider branching into related niches or promoting different types of products. Expanding your range of topics or offerings can attract a wider range of visitors.

4. Build a Team:
As your business grows, you might need assistance with content creation, social media management, or customer support. Hiring freelancers or collaborators can help you scale efficiently.

5. Invest in Paid Advertising:
Consider investing in paid advertising, such as social media ads or Google Ads. Paid ads can

amplify your reach and target specific audience segments.

6. Develop Automation Systems:
Implement automation tools for tasks like email marketing, social media scheduling, and analytics tracking. Automation frees up your time for strategic planning.

7. Collaborate and Network:
Build relationships with fellow affiliates, influencers, and brands in your niche. Collaborations and partnerships can expose you to new audiences and opportunities.

8. Offer Premium Content:
Consider offering premium content or membership options to your audience. This can provide an additional revenue stream and attract dedicated followers.

9. Explore New Promotion Channels:

Research and experiment with new promotion channels. For example, if you've been primarily using blogs, consider expanding into podcasts or webinars.

10. Create Evergreen Content:

Focus on creating evergreen content that remains relevant over time. This type of content continues to attract traffic and generate affiliate revenue long after it's published.

11. Attend Industry Events:

Participate in conferences, webinars, and industry events to stay updated on trends and connect with other professionals in your field.

12. Monitor Data and Analytics:

Regularly analyze your data and metrics to identify trends, areas for improvement, and new opportunities. Data-driven decisions are crucial for effective scaling.

13. Offer Incentives:

Incentivize your audience to refer others or share your content. Referral programs or rewards for sharing can help you expand your reach organically.

14. Stay Committed to Quality:

As you scale, maintain the quality of your content and recommendations. Consistency and credibility are essential for retaining your audience's trust.

15. Be Patient and Adaptive:

Scaling takes time. Be patient and willing to adapt your strategies based on the results you see. Continuously refine your approach to achieve sustainable growth.

Scaling your affiliate business requires careful planning, dedication, and ongoing effort. By implementing these strategies and staying focused on delivering value to your audience, you can successfully expand your reach, increase revenue, and achieve long-term success in affiliate marketing.

Analyzing Performance Metrics

Analyzing performance metrics is crucial for assessing the effectiveness of your affiliate marketing efforts and making informed decisions to optimize your strategy. Here are key performance metrics to monitor and how to interpret them:

1. Click-Through Rate (CTR):
CTR measures the percentage of people who clicked on your affiliate links compared to the total number of impressions. A higher CTR indicates that your content is compelling and driving engagement.

2. Conversion Rate:
Conversion rate calculates the percentage of visitors who took the desired action, such as making a purchase or signing up, compared to

the total number of visitors. A higher conversion rate indicates effective targeting and persuasive content.

3. Earnings per Click (EPC):
EPC represents the average earnings generated per click on your affiliate links. It's calculated by dividing your total earnings by the total number of clicks. A higher EPC suggests that your links are leading to higher-quality traffic and conversions.

4. Average Order Value (AOV):
AOV measures the average amount spent by customers on each transaction. A higher AOV indicates that your audience is purchasing more valuable products.

5. Return on Investment (ROI):

ROI assesses the profitability of your affiliate campaigns by comparing the revenue earned to the costs invested (e.g., advertising expenses). A positive ROI indicates a successful campaign.

6. Bounce Rate:

Bounce rate measures the percentage of visitors who leave your website after viewing only one page. A high bounce rate could suggest that your content doesn't align with user expectations.

7. Time on Page:

Time on page indicates how long visitors spend on a specific page. Higher time on page suggests that your content is engaging and relevant.

8. Subscriber Growth Rate:

For email marketing, monitor how quickly your subscriber list is growing. A steady growth rate indicates that your content and offers are resonating with your audience.

9. Social Engagement Metrics:
Track likes, shares, comments, and retweets on social media. High engagement signals that your content is resonating and encouraging interaction.

10. Churn Rate:
In subscription-based affiliate programs, churn rate measures the rate at which customers cancel or unsubscribe. A lower churn rate indicates customer satisfaction and retention.

11. Traffic Sources:

Identify where your website traffic is coming from. This helps you understand which promotion channels are most effective.

12. Affiliate Link Performance:
Monitor which affiliate links generate the most clicks and conversions. Focus on promoting products that resonate with your audience.

13. Geographic and Demographic Data:
Analyze the geographic locations and demographics of your audience. This information helps you tailor content and promotions to specific segments.

14. Cart Abandonment Rate:
For e-commerce affiliates, track how often users abandon their shopping carts before completing a purchase. Identifying reasons for

abandonment can help you optimize the conversion process.

15. A/B Testing Results:
If you're running A/B tests, compare the performance of different variations. This helps you understand which elements resonate best with your audience.

Regularly monitoring these performance metrics provides insights into the effectiveness of your affiliate marketing efforts. Analyze trends, identify areas for improvement, and adapt your strategy accordingly to achieve optimal results.

Ethical and Legal Considerations

Ethical and legal considerations are paramount in affiliate marketing. Adhering to ethical standards and legal regulations not only protects your credibility but also maintains the trust of your audience and affiliate partners. Here's a guide to navigate the ethical and legal aspects of affiliate marketing:

Ethical Considerations:

- Transparency: Always disclose your affiliate relationships and any compensation you receive when promoting products. Transparency builds trust with your audience.
- Honesty: Provide accurate and unbiased information about the products you're

promoting. Avoid exaggerations or misleading claims.

- Genuine Recommendations: Only promote products you believe in or have personally used. Recommending products solely for profit can damage your reputation.
- Value-Centered Content: Focus on delivering value to your audience. Create content that educates, informs, and solves problems rather than simply pushing products.
- Respect Audience Privacy: Obtain consent when collecting personal information, and adhere to data protection laws. Safeguard your audience's privacy.
- Quality Over Quantity: Prioritize quality content over excessive promotion.

Overloading your audience with affiliate links can lead to disengagement.

- Avoid Plagiarism: Create original content. Plagiarism not only damages your credibility but can also result in legal consequences.

Legal Considerations:

- FTC Disclosure: The Federal Trade Commission (FTC) in the U.S. mandates that you disclose your affiliate relationships clearly and conspicuously. Use clear language that your audience can understand.
- Cookie Consent: If your website uses cookies, obtain consent from visitors in compliance with cookie laws like GDPR in the European Union.
- Copyright Laws: Respect copyright laws when using images, videos, and other

content. Obtain proper permissions or use royalty-free content.

- Endorsement Guidelines: Adhere to endorsement guidelines outlined by the FTC. Clearly state if you've received products for free or are being compensated for your review.

- Trademark Usage: Be cautious when using trademarks in your content. Unauthorized use can lead to legal issues.

- Affiliate Agreements: Read and understand the terms of your affiliate agreements. Some programs may have specific requirements or restrictions.

- Geographical Regulations: Be aware of regulations in different regions. For example, the General Data Protection Regulation (GDPR) affects how you collect and process data from EU citizens.

- Tax Obligations: Understand your tax obligations related to affiliate income. Consult with a tax professional to ensure compliance.
- Product Claims: Avoid making false or unsubstantiated claims about the products you're promoting. Stick to accurate and verifiable information.
- Unsolicited Emails: If you're using email marketing, comply with anti-spam laws such as the CAN-SPAM Act in the U.S. and similar laws in other regions.

Staying ethical and compliant not only protects you legally but also maintains the trust and loyalty of your audience. Familiarize yourself with the relevant laws and guidelines in your region, and prioritize honesty, transparency, and providing genuine value in your affiliate marketing endeavors.

Disclosure and Transparency Guidelines

Disclosure and transparency are essential aspects of ethical affiliate marketing. Clearly informing your audience about your affiliate relationships builds trust and maintains your credibility. Here are guidelines for effective disclosure and transparency:

1. Clear and Conspicuous Language:
Use language that is easy to understand and prominently placed. Disclosures should be visible and not buried in small print.

2. Early Placement:
Place disclosures near the beginning of your content, whether it's a blog post, video, or social media post. This ensures that your audience is aware of your affiliation from the start.

3. Use of Labels:

Use labels such as "Affiliate," "Sponsored," "Paid Promotion," or "Ad" to clearly indicate that you're earning from the promotion.

4. Positioning in Social Media Posts:

In social media, ensure that your disclosure appears within the first few lines of the post, where it's less likely to be cut off.

5. Use of Hashtags:

When applicable, use hashtags like #ad, #sponsored, or #affiliate in your posts to indicate the promotional nature of the content.

6. Consistency Across Platforms:

Maintain consistency in your disclosure practices across all platforms and content types.

7. Specificity of Relationships:

Specify your relationship with the brand or product. For example, mention if you received free products, compensation, or if it's a genuine recommendation.

8. Transparency in Reviews:
Clearly state whether you've personally used the product or service you're reviewing. Authenticity in your reviews is crucial.

9. Visual Disclosures:
If using images or videos, include a disclosure in the visual content itself or as part of the caption.

10. Transparency in Affiliate Links:
Notify users when a link is an affiliate link by including a statement in close proximity to the link. For example, "This link is an affiliate link."

11. Update Disclosures:

If your relationship with a brand or product changes, update your disclosures accordingly.

12. Tone of Disclosure:

Maintain a straightforward and informative tone in your disclosures. Avoid language that may confuse or mislead your audience.

13. Consideration of Platform Limitations:

Be aware of space limitations on certain platforms, like character limits on social media. Adapt your disclosure to fit within these constraints.

14. Align with FTC Guidelines:

Adhere to disclosure guidelines outlined by the Federal Trade Commission (FTC) or relevant regulatory bodies in your region.

15. Educate Your Audience:

Educate your audience about what your disclosures mean and why they are important. This helps build understanding and trust.

Remember that the goal of disclosure and transparency is to ensure your audience is fully aware of your affiliate relationships. By being open about your affiliations and providing clear information, you build a foundation of trust that can strengthen your relationship with your audience over time.

Avoiding Common Affiliate Marketing Pitfalls

Avoiding common affiliate marketing pitfalls is essential for maintaining your reputation, credibility, and long-term success. Here are some pitfalls to be aware of and how to steer clear of them:

1. Promoting Low-Quality Products:
Avoid promoting products solely for the sake of earning commissions. Focus on products that genuinely provide value to your audience and align with your niche.

2. Lack of Transparency:
Always disclose your affiliate relationships clearly and conspicuously. Transparency builds trust with your audience and prevents potential legal issues.

3. Overpromotion and Spamming:

Excessive promotion or spammy tactics can alienate your audience. Prioritize delivering valuable content over bombarding them with affiliate links.

4. Ignoring Your Audience's Needs:

Understand your audience's pain points and interests. Ignoring their needs can lead to disengagement and a loss of credibility.

5. Not Researching Affiliate Programs:

Before joining an affiliate program, thoroughly research the product, company, and compensation structure. Choose reputable programs with products you can stand behind.

6. Neglecting to Test Products:

Promoting products without testing them can lead to recommending subpar items. Test and experience products before promoting them to ensure their quality.

7. Overlooking Legal Compliance:
Failure to adhere to legal regulations, such as FTC guidelines, can result in legal consequences and damage your reputation. Familiarize yourself with the laws in your region.

8. Relying Solely on One Traffic Source:
Diversify your traffic sources to reduce dependency on one platform. Changes in algorithms or policies can impact your reach overnight.

9. Neglecting Mobile Responsiveness:
With mobile users on the rise, ensure that your website and content are mobile-responsive. A

poor mobile experience can lead to high bounce rates.

10. Not Monitoring Performance Metrics:
Regularly analyze performance metrics to track your progress and identify areas for improvement. Data-driven decisions lead to better outcomes.

11. Ignoring Feedback:
Pay attention to feedback from your audience. Address concerns, answer questions, and use feedback to refine your approach.

12. Not Adapting to Trends:
Staying stagnant and ignoring industry trends can cause your strategies to become outdated. Continuously adapt to changes in the affiliate marketing landscape.

13. Chasing Short-Term Gains:
Focus on building long-term relationships with your audience. Prioritize providing value over quick profits.

14. Poor Time Management:
Efficient time management is crucial in affiliate marketing. Plan your tasks, set goals, and allocate time for content creation, promotion, and analysis.

15. Impatience:
Affiliate marketing takes time to yield significant results. Avoid becoming discouraged if you don't see immediate success. Stay patient and consistent.

By being aware of these pitfalls and taking proactive steps to avoid them, you can navigate the world of affiliate marketing with integrity, professionalism, and a focus on delivering value to your audience.

Staying Compliant with FTC Regulations

Staying compliant with Federal Trade Commission (FTC) regulations is essential for maintaining transparency, credibility, and legal integrity in your affiliate marketing efforts. Here's how to ensure you're adhering to FTC guidelines:

1. Disclose Your Affiliate Relationship:
Clearly disclose your relationship with the brands and products you're promoting. Use clear and conspicuous language that your audience can easily understand.

2. Prominent Placement of Disclosures:
Place disclosures where they're easily noticeable, such as at the beginning of blog posts, videos, or social media captions.

3. Use Specific Disclosure Labels:

Use disclosure labels like "Ad," "Sponsored," "Paid Promotion," or "Affiliate" to convey that your content includes affiliate links or sponsored content.

4. Tone of Disclosures:

Make your disclosures straightforward and unambiguous. Avoid vague language that might confuse your audience.

5. Applicable to All Platforms:

Ensure that your disclosure practices are consistent across all platforms where you promote affiliate products, including social media, websites, and email marketing.

6. Single Click Access:

Ensure that your audience can access your disclosures with a single click. Don't bury them behind multiple links or layers of navigation.

7. Affiliation with Products:
Clearly communicate whether you've used the products you're promoting. Authenticity in your recommendations builds trust.

8. Updates for Material Connections:
If your relationship with a brand or product changes, update your disclosures accordingly to reflect the current status.

9. Compliance for Endorsements:
If you provide endorsements or testimonials, they must reflect your honest opinions and experiences. Avoid making false or misleading claims.

10. Use of Affiliate Links:

Clearly indicate that a link is an affiliate link, either through a disclosure near the link or by using clear labeling on the link itself.

11. Educate Your Audience:

Help your audience understand the importance of disclosures. Educate them about why you're providing disclosures and how they benefit from them.

12. Stay Updated on Regulations:

Keep up to date with any changes in FTC guidelines related to affiliate marketing. Guidelines may evolve, so staying informed is crucial.

13. Training for Your Team:

If you have a team assisting with your affiliate marketing efforts, ensure they understand FTC guidelines and are aligned with your compliance practices.

14. Seek Legal Advice if Unsure:
If you're unsure about how to properly disclose or comply with FTC regulations, consult legal counsel for guidance.

15. Prioritize Transparency:
Above all, prioritize transparency and honesty in your affiliate marketing endeavors. Being transparent not only keeps you compliant but also fosters trust with your audience.

By consistently following these guidelines, you can ensure that your affiliate marketing practices are ethical, transparent, and compliant with FTC regulations. This approach not only protects you from potential legal issues but also maintains the trust and loyalty of your audience.

Future Trends in Affiliate Marketing

Affiliate marketing continues to evolve as technology and consumer behavior change. Here are some future trends to watch in the world of affiliate marketing:

1. Influencer Partnerships: Collaborations between influencers and brands will become more common. Brands will partner with influencers who have genuine connections with their target audiences.

2. Voice Search Optimization: As voice search usage grows, optimizing content for voice search will become crucial. Long-tail keywords and natural language will play a more significant role.

3. Video Content Dominance: Video content, including live streaming and short-form videos, will continue to dominate. Video is a powerful way to engage audiences and showcase products.

4. AI and Automation: Artificial intelligence (AI) and automation will streamline tasks such as content distribution, audience targeting, and data analysis, making campaigns more efficient.

5. Niche and Micro-Influencers: Brands will focus on working with niche and micro-influencers who have smaller but highly engaged audiences. These influencers often yield more authentic results.

6. Diversification of Affiliate Products: Affiliates will diversify the types of products they promote, moving beyond physical products to

digital goods, online courses, and subscription services.

7. Personalization and Segmentation: Affiliates will leverage data to personalize content and promotions for specific segments of their audience, enhancing engagement and conversions.

8. Enhanced Tracking and Attribution: Improved tracking mechanisms will provide affiliates with better insights into customer journeys, allowing for more accurate attribution and optimization.

9. Sustainable and Ethical Marketing: There will be a greater emphasis on promoting sustainable and ethical products. Consumers are more conscious of their choices, and brands will align with these values.

10. Mobile-Centric Strategies: With mobile usage on the rise, affiliates will adopt mobile-centric strategies, including mobile-responsive websites, mobile apps, and mobile-specific promotions.

11. Interactive Content: Interactive content like quizzes, polls, and interactive product demos will engage audiences and encourage participation, driving conversions.

12. AI-Powered Content Creation: AI tools will assist in content creation, generating data-driven insights to help affiliates create more relevant and effective content.

13. Subscription and Membership Models: Affiliates may explore promoting subscription and membership models, as these offer

recurring revenue streams and customer retention.

14. Virtual Reality (VR) and Augmented Reality (AR): As VR and AR technology advances, affiliates may use these immersive experiences to showcase products in unique ways.

15. Cross-Channel Consistency: Maintaining a consistent brand presence across various channels, from social media to email marketing, will be crucial for building trust and recognition.

Staying adaptable and open to embracing new technologies and strategies will be key to thriving in the evolving landscape of affiliate marketing. As consumer preferences shift and technology advances, affiliates who stay ahead of the curve will be better positioned for success.

Emerging Technologies and Their Impact

Emerging technologies are reshaping the affiliate marketing landscape, offering new opportunities and challenges for affiliates. Here's a look at some of these technologies and their potential impact:

1. Artificial Intelligence (AI):
AI is revolutionizing affiliate marketing by enabling data-driven insights, predictive analytics, and personalized recommendations. AI-powered tools can help affiliates optimize content, target audiences more effectively, and even automate certain tasks.

2. Voice Search and Voice Assistants:
The rise of voice search and voice assistants like Siri and Alexa is changing how people search

for and discover products. Affiliates will need to adapt their content to be voice-search friendly and consider voice-based affiliate partnerships.

3. Augmented Reality (AR) and Virtual Reality (VR):

AR and VR are transforming product experiences. Affiliates can leverage these technologies to create immersive demonstrations, allowing customers to interact with products virtually before making a purchase.

4. Blockchain and Cryptocurrency:

Blockchain technology can enhance transparency and security in affiliate marketing by providing verifiable transaction records. Cryptocurrency payments might become a viable option for affiliate commissions, offering faster and borderless transactions.

5. Chatbots and Conversational AI:

Chatbots and conversational AI are enhancing customer interactions. Affiliates can use chatbots to engage with visitors, answer questions, and guide them toward relevant products.

6. 5G Connectivity:

Faster 5G connectivity will enable better mobile experiences, including quicker loading times for content and smoother video streaming. Affiliates should optimize their content for this improved mobile experience.

7. Data Privacy Tools:

With growing concerns about data privacy, tools that offer better control over personal data will become important. Affiliates will need to ensure they are compliant with privacy regulations and communicate their privacy practices clearly.

8. Predictive Analytics:
Predictive analytics can help affiliates anticipate trends, customer behavior, and market changes. This insight enables more strategic content creation and promotional efforts.

9. Social Commerce Integration:
Social media platforms are integrating shopping features, making it easier for users to make purchases without leaving the platform. Affiliates can tap into this trend by creating shoppable content.

10. Personalization Engines:
Advanced personalization engines allow affiliates to tailor content and product recommendations to individual user

preferences, enhancing user experience and increasing conversions.

11. Internet of Things (IoT):

The IoT can create new affiliate opportunities, such as promoting smart home devices. Affiliates might focus on how these devices simplify users' lives and integrate into their routines.

12. Wearable Technology:

Wearable devices open up possibilities for targeted promotions based on users' health and lifestyle data. Affiliates can align with health and fitness brands to leverage this trend.

13. Biometric Authentication:

As security becomes more important, biometric authentication methods like fingerprint recognition and facial scanning could influence how affiliates engage with audiences.

14. Visual Search:
Visual search allows users to search using images. Affiliates can optimize images and leverage visual search tools to connect users with relevant products.

15. Emphasis on Sustainability and Ethical Tech: As consumers become more conscious of sustainability, affiliates might focus on promoting eco-friendly products and technologies.

Staying informed about emerging technologies and their implications for affiliate marketing can give you a competitive edge. By adapting your strategies to incorporate these trends, you can create more engaging and effective campaigns for your audience.

Lessons Learned from Top Affiliate Marketers

Top affiliate marketers have valuable insights that can guide aspiring affiliates toward success. Here are some key lessons learned from top affiliate marketers:

1. Focus on Audience Value:
Top affiliates prioritize delivering value to their audience above all else. They focus on solving problems, providing information, and addressing their audience's needs.

2. Build Trust and Credibility:
Establishing trust and credibility is crucial. Successful affiliates are transparent, honest, and build genuine relationships with their audience.

3. Test and Optimize:

Constantly test different strategies, content formats, and promotional methods. Top affiliates analyze data to identify what works best and continuously optimize their approach.

4. Quality Over Quantity:

Rather than pushing numerous products, top affiliates emphasize quality over quantity. They promote products they believe in and would genuinely recommend to their audience.

5. Diversify Promotion Channels:

Top affiliates diversify their promotion channels, from blogs and social media to email marketing and podcasts. This widens their reach and minimizes risk from platform changes.

6. Know Your Niche:

Deeply understand your niche and target audience. Top affiliates tailor their content and recommendations to resonate with their specific audience's interests and preferences.

7. Persistence and Patience:
Building a successful affiliate marketing business takes time. Top affiliates emphasize persistence, consistency, and the patience to see results over the long term.

8. Adapt to Changes:
The affiliate marketing landscape evolves. Top affiliates stay updated on industry trends, algorithm changes, and emerging technologies, adapting their strategies accordingly.

9. Focus on Relationships:
Building relationships with both your audience and affiliate partners is key. Top affiliates foster

strong relationships that lead to mutual trust and beneficial collaborations.

10. Continuous Learning:

Affiliate marketing is always evolving. Top affiliates dedicate time to learning about new strategies, tools, and techniques to stay ahead of the curve.

11. Data-Driven Decisions:

Top affiliates rely on data to make informed decisions. They analyze performance metrics to understand what's working and adjust their strategies accordingly.

12. Be Unique and Authentic:

Differentiate yourself from the competition by showcasing your unique personality and perspective. Authenticity helps you stand out and connect with your audience.

13. Persevere Through Challenges:

Challenges are part of the journey. Top affiliates persevere through setbacks, learning from failures, and using them to fuel their growth.

14. Prioritize User Experience:

A seamless and enjoyable user experience is essential. Top affiliates ensure that their websites are user-friendly, mobile-responsive, and easy to navigate.

15. Focus on Long-Term Goals:

Top affiliates avoid shortcuts and prioritize building a sustainable business. They're not solely driven by quick gains but rather by building a lasting brand.

By embracing these lessons from top affiliate marketers, you can develop a solid foundation for your own affiliate marketing journey and increase your chances of achieving success in the long run.

Conclusion

In conclusion, affiliate marketing offers a dynamic and rewarding opportunity to earn income by promoting products and services you believe in. Throughout this guide, we've explored the fundamental aspects of affiliate marketing, from understanding its history to mastering key strategies for success.

Remember that affiliate marketing requires dedication, continuous learning, and a commitment to delivering value to your audience. By choosing the right products, building trust, creating compelling content, and utilizing various promotional techniques, you can establish a thriving affiliate business.

Stay informed about industry trends, adapt to emerging technologies, and prioritize ethical practices and compliance with regulations. Building authentic relationships with your audience and affiliate partners will be essential for sustainable growth.

As you embark on your affiliate marketing journey, keep in mind that success doesn't happen overnight. Patience, perseverance, and a willingness to learn from both successes and setbacks will be your allies. So go forth with confidence, armed with the knowledge and strategies you've gained, and make your mark in the world of affiliate marketing. Good luck!